The Joy of Baroque

Selected and edited by Denes Agay

Keyboard literature of the Baroque, created roughly between 1600 and 1750, is perhaps the richest and most varied of any period. Numerous areas of this vast and delightful world of keyboard music are still largely excluded from the teaching repertory of the piano student mainly because of the scarcity of easily available, reliable editions. The purpose of this volume is to provide the student, the teacher and any interested player with a collection of appealing works by these neglected Baroque masters, Pachelbel, Kindermann, Zipoli, Pescetti, Soler, just to mention a few. These writers created a profusion of appealing small keyboard works which are utterly melodic, clear in texture and, in most cases, also easier than the Bach Inventions. This volume also contains rarely encountered charming works by the giants of the period, Handel, Bach, Couperin, Telemann, and others.

All works herein are in their original forms, based on authentic texts. Editorial additions are either in small print or referred to in footnotes. The grade level is easy-to-intermediate, in an approximately progressive sequence.

When performing the keyboard music of the Baroque the following suggestions may be kept in mind:

—Tempo is generally steady; excessive speed should be avoided; small retards in concluding measures may be taken for granted.

—Legato, non-legato and staccato touches are all acceptable if employed with intelligent consistency within a piece.

—Extreme dynamic contrasts should be avoided; the range is between piano and forte and not between pianissimo and fortissimo.

—Pedal should be used sparingly, mostly in "short touches", or not at all.

—In performing Baroque music sentimentality is out of place, but *expressiveness* is not. The player should not be hampered by the pedantic application of half-assimilated rules; neither should he be intimidated by rigid, hair-splitting pronouncements on stylistic purity. The performer of the 17th and 18th centuries had a great deal of freedom, fully sanctioned by the Baroque composer who did not indicate the details and nuances of execution in his manuscripts, but left them to the discretion and good taste of the player.

International Standard Book Number: 0.8256.8015.8
Library of Congress Catalog Card Number: 74-83439

Exclusive Distributors:
Music Sales Corporation
225 Park Avenue South, New York, NY 10003
Music Sales Limited
8/9 Frith Street, London W1V 5TZ England
Music Sales Pty. Limited
120 Rothschild Street, Rosebery, Sydney, NSW 2018, Australia

Printed in the United States of America

Contents

4 Menuet
Johann Krieger

5 Menuet
Johann Kuhnau

6 Allemande
Johann Herrmann Schein

6 Aria
Daniel Speer

7 Gavotto
Daniel Speer

8 Menuet
Johann Heinrich Buttstedt

9 Sarabanda
Johann Erasmus Kindermann

10 Preambulum
Unknown Composer

11 Gavotte
Gottlieb Muffat

12 Aria Pastorella—*Dance of the Shepherds*
Valentin Rathgeber

14 Folia—*Folies d'Espagne*
Alessandro Scarlatti

17 Air—*from a Sonata in A minor*
John Christopher Pepusch

18 A Ground In Gamut
Henry Purcell

21 March
Henry Purcell

22 Theatre Tune
John Blow

23 Prelude—*from a Partita For Young People*
Johann Nikolaus Tischer

24 Fughetta
George Frideric Handel

26 Canzone
George Frideric Handel

28 Minuetto with Variations
Giovanni Battista Martini

30 Presto—*from a Sonata for Harpsichord*
Giovanni Battista Pescetti

33 Polonaise
Johann Philipp Kirnberger

34 Allegro
Georg Philipp Telemann

35 Scherzino
Georg Philipp Telemann

36 Polonaise
Johann Gottlieb Goldberg

37 Divertimento
Mattia Vento

40 Gavotta
Domenico Zipoli

42 Two Sonatinas—*from Six Sonatine Nuove*
Carl Philipp Emanuel Bach

44 Toccata—*First Movement*
Carlos Seixas

46 March
Johann Christoph Friedrich Bach

48 Chaconne
Johann Pachelbel

51 Versetto—*(Fughetta)*
Domenico Zipoli

52 Lament—*from Capriccio*
Johann Sebastian Bach

54 Courante—*from a Sonata in D minor*
Johann Gottlieb Graun

57 Trio—*from a Minuet in F*
Johann Christoph Friedrich Bach

58 L'Indiscrete—*Rondeau*
Jean Philippe Rameau

60 Sonata
George Frideric Handel

62 La Bouffonne—*from Ordre No. 20*
François Couperin

64 Sonata
Antonio Soler

68 Rondeau
Friedrich Wilhelm Marpurg

70 La Complaisante
Carl Philipp Emanuel Bach

72 Fantasia
Georg Philipp Telemann

75 La Lutine—*The Impish Girl*
Johann Philipp Kirnberger

76 Sonata—*L. 93*
Domenico Scarlatti

78 Toccata
Leonardo Leo

Menuet

Johann Krieger
(1651-1735)

Menuet

Johann Kuhnau
(1660- 1722)

Allemande

Johann Herrmann Schein
(1586—1630)

Aria

Daniel Speer
(1636—1707)

＊ For easier reading note values were doubled.

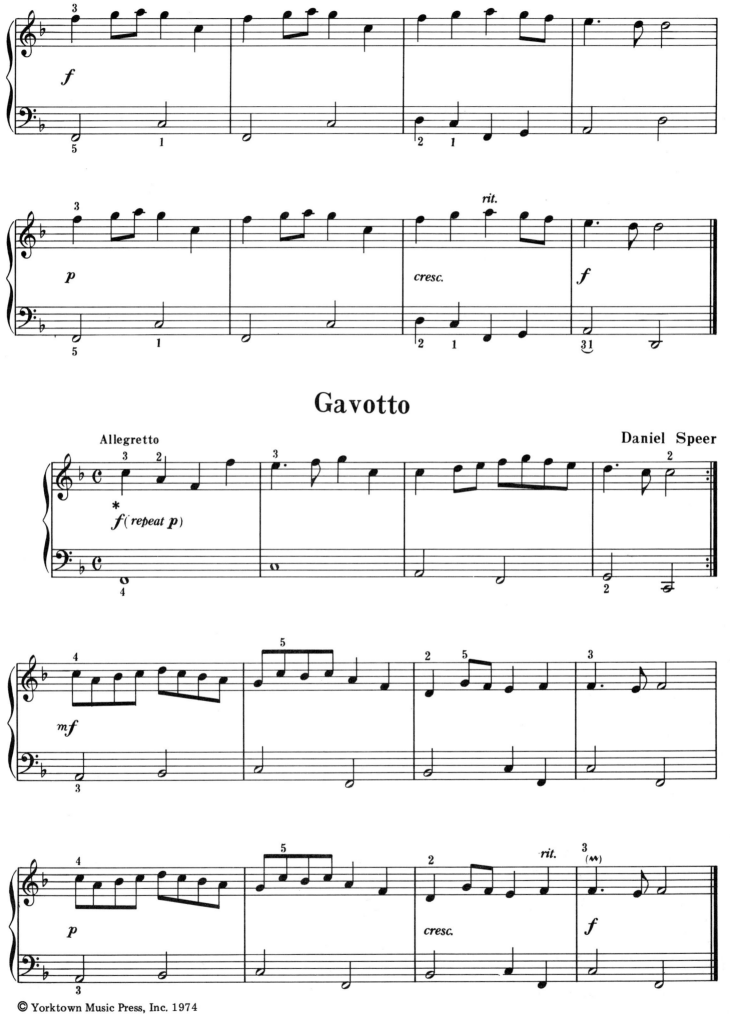

Gavotto

Daniel Speer

Allegretto

* f (repeat p)

* Note values are doubled.

Menuet

Johann Heinrich Buttstedt
(1666—1727)

Sarabanda

Johann Erasmus Kindermann
(1616- 1655)

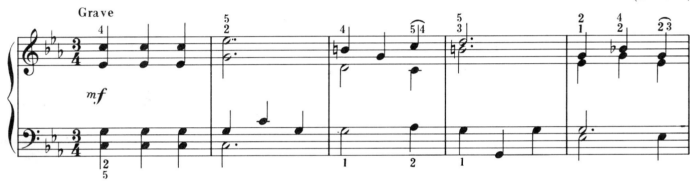

Preambulum

Unknown composer
(around 1730)

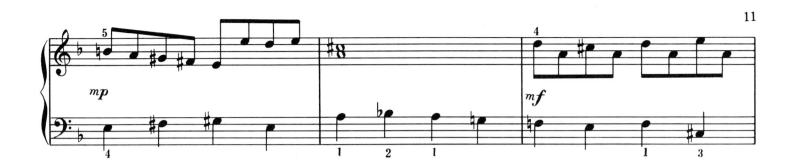

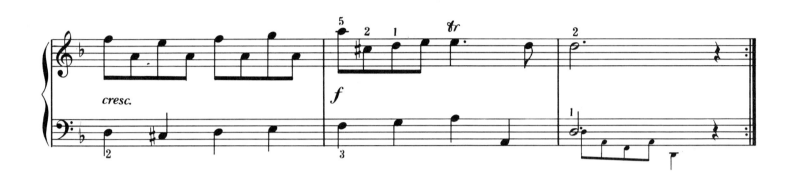

Gavotte

Gottlieb Muffat
(1690- 1770)

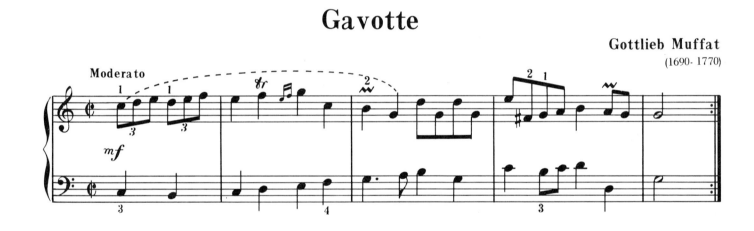

Aria Pastorella

Dance of the Shepherds

Valentin Rathgeber
(1682- 1750)

D. C. al Fine

Folia
Folies d'Espagne

Alessandro Scarlatti
(1660- 1725)

4.

Air
from a Sonata in A minor

John Christopher Pepusch
(1667- 1752)

* Small notes are editorial additions, based on the composer's figured bass.

D. C. al Fine

A Ground In Gamut

Henry Purcell
(1659- 1695)

Andante cantabile

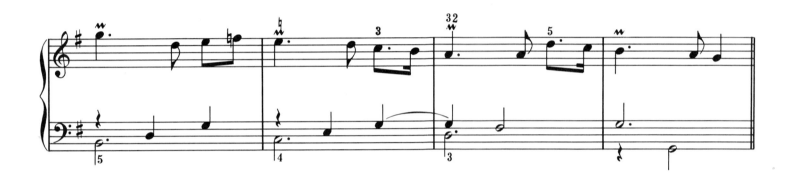

✱ *Ground* is one of the oldest versions of the variation form: a persistently repeated unchanging melody line in the bass with varied upper parts. *Gamut* originally meant the note G on the bottom line of the bass clef. It also came to mean a scale, particularly in the key of G.

March

Henry Purcell

Andante con moto

Theatre Tune

John Blow
(1648- 1708)

Prelude
from a Partita For Young People

Johann Nikolaus Tischer
(1731- 1767)

Fughetta

George Frideric Handel
(1685-1759)

Canzone*

George Frideric Handel

*From an 18th century manuscript collection.

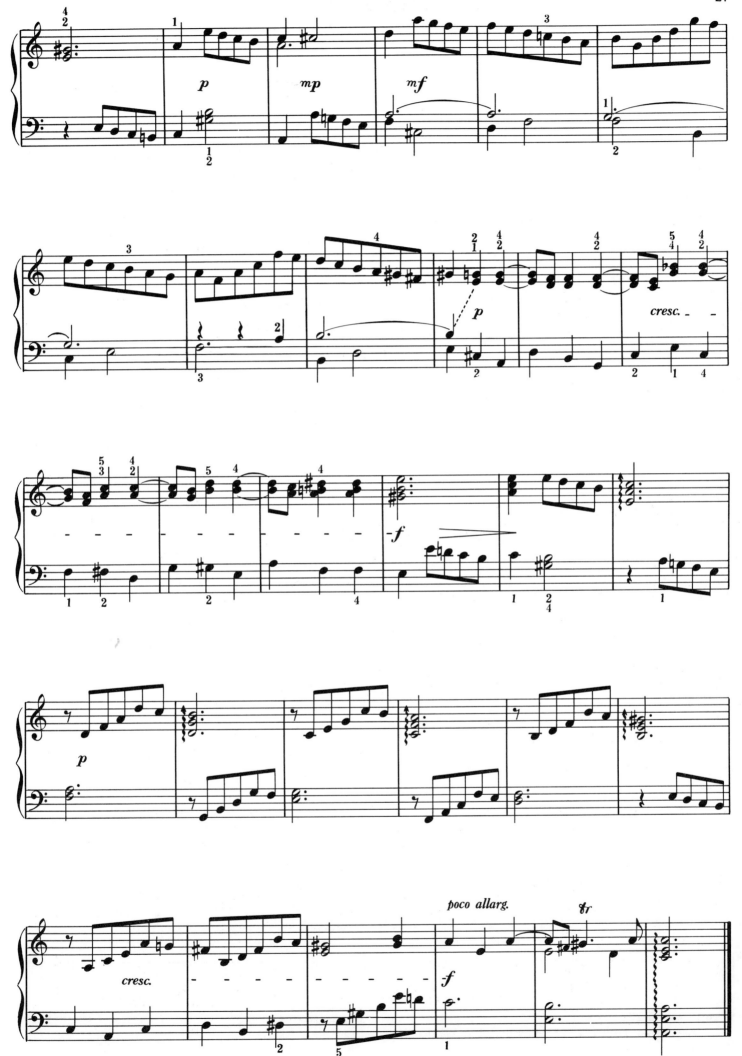

Minuetto with Variations

Giovanni Battista Martini
(1706-1784)

Andante grazioso

Presto
from a Sonata for Harpsichord

Giovanni Battista Pescetti
(1704-1766)

Polonaise

Johann   Philipp   Kirnberger
(1721-1783)

Allegro

Georg Philipp Telemann
(1681- 1767)

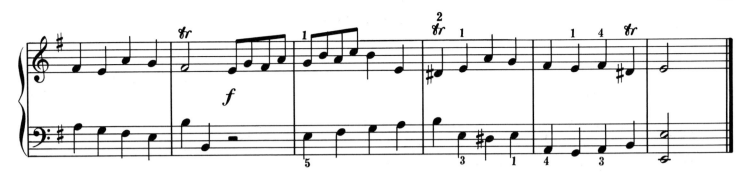

Scherzino

Allegretto

Georg Philipp Telemann

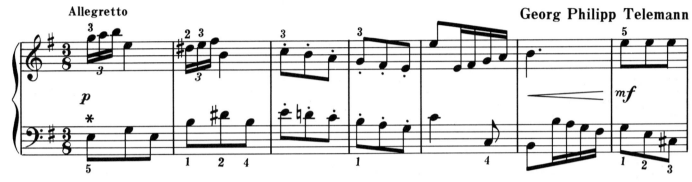

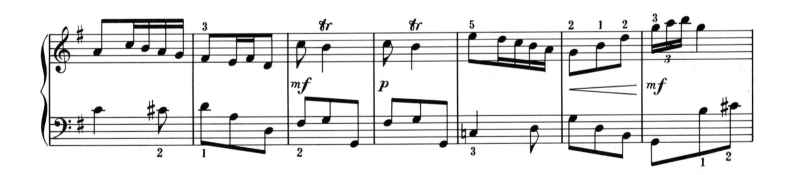

*All eighth notes may be played staccato, unless indicated otherwise.

Polonaise

Johann Gottlieb Goldberg
(1727-1756)

Divertimento

Mattia Vento
(1735- 1776)

Gavotta

Domenico Zipoli
(1688-1726)

Two Sonatinas

from Six Sonatine Nuove

Carl Philipp Emanuel Bach
(1714- 1788)

Toccata
First Movement

Carlos Seixas
(1704-1742)

Allegro

* Unless suggested otherwise, all eighth notes may be played staccato.

(2nd time allargando)

March

Johann Christoph Friedrich Bach
(1732- 1795)

Moderato con moto

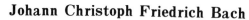
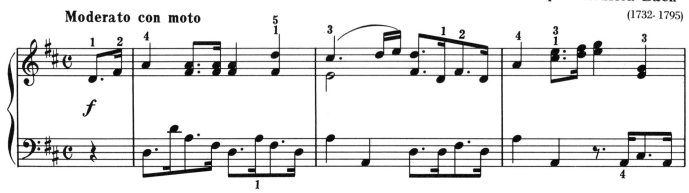

Chaconne

Johann Pachelbel
(1653 1706)

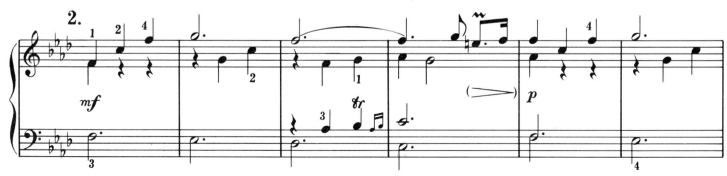

Versetto
(Fughetta)

Domenico Zipoli
(1688- 1726)

Moderato

Lament
from "Capriccio"
(Describing the departure of his beloved brother)

Johann Sebastian Bach
(1685- 1750)

* Small notes are editorial additions based on Bach's figured bass.

Courante
from a Sonata in D minor

Johann Gottlieb Graun
(1703-1771)

Trio
from a Minuet in F

Johann Christoph Friedrich Bach
(1732-1795)

Andante

L'Indiscrete
Rondeau

Jean Philippe Rameau
(1683- 1764)

Vivement

Sonata

George Frideric Handel
(1685-1759)

La Bouffonne

from Ordre No. 20

François Couperin
(1668- 1733)

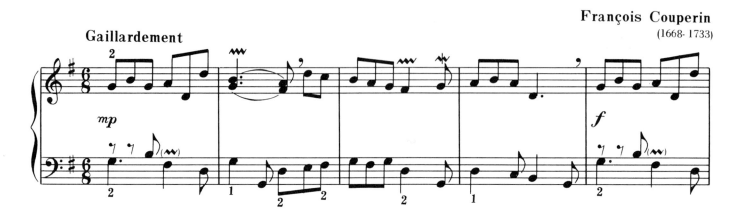

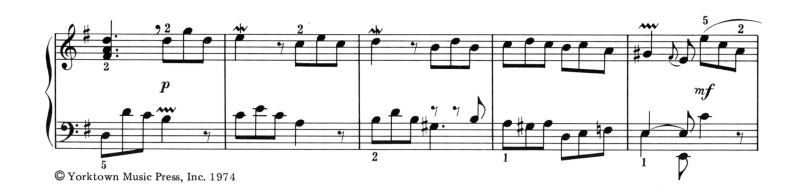

Sonata

Antonio Soler
(1729-1783)

Rondeau

I

Friedrich Wilhelm Marpurg
(1718- 1795)

Allegretto grazioso

D. C. al Fine
senza repetizione

II

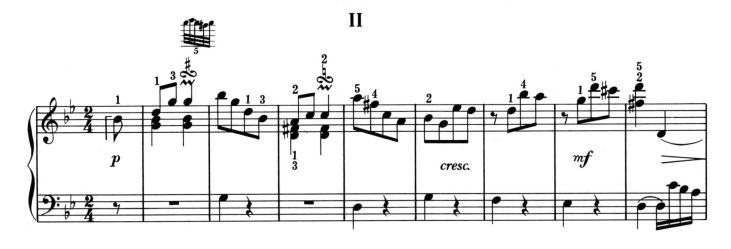

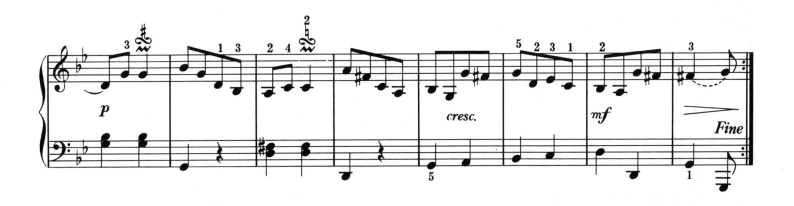

D. C. al Fine
e poi D. C. Rondeau I.

La Complaisante

Carl Philipp Emanuel Bach
(1714- 1788)

Fantasia

Georg Philipp Telemann
(1681- 1767)

Repeat Allegro

La Lutine

The Impish Girl

Johann Philipp Kirnberger
(1721-1782)

* All eighth-notes may be played staccato.

Sonata
L. 93

Domenico Scarlatti
(1685- 1757)

Toccata

Leonardo Leo
(1694-1744)